How to Make Money on TikTok in 2024

The Complete Guide for Businesses, Creators, and Influencers

The Fix-It Guy

Copyright © The Fix-It Guy

Table of Contents

Introduction

Hello, TikTok fans, businesses, and aspiring influencers! Have you ever wondered what it takes to ride the TikTok viral wave and transform those addicting scrolling sessions into real money? Hold on to your iPhones, because I have something wonderful in store for you!

TikTok is the undisputed king of creativity and immediate celebrity in the explosive world of social media, where trends are formed in seconds and viral videos can make you an overnight sensation. You're in for a treat if you're a company owner looking to expand your brand's reach, a content producer seeking popularity, or simply someone who enjoys scrolling endlessly through intriguing material.

Consider this: You, easily generate material that not only entertains the TikTok cosmos but also fills your bank account. Imagine converting your love for dancing, cooking, or simply being yourself into a profitable business while having fun. Is it too wonderful to be true? That's not the case, my friend.

We're going deep into the core of TikTok in 2024 in the pages of this book. It's not just another guide; it's your passport to uncovering the secrets of TikTok's success, customized for this dynamic, ever-changing platform.

We'll decipher the algorithms, unearth the trends, and uncover the methods that can help your video content stand out in a sea of videos.

But here's the greatest part: you don't need a professional camera crew or a marketing degree. All you need is a little imagination, a smartphone, and a willingness to learn. This book is your compass in the tumultuous world of viral content and digital enterprise, whether you're a tech-savvy kid, a seasoned entrepreneur, or someone who's just jumped on the TikTok bandwagon.

So, are you ready to transform your addicting TikTok hours into a successful business, a thriving brand, or a powerful online presence? If you answered "YES!" then strap in, for the journey of a lifetime awaits you within these pages. Let's make 2024 the year that your TikTok fantasies come true. Let's start browsing, making stuff, and, most importantly, cashing in!

Chapter 1

Getting Started on TikTok

Creating a TikTok Account

Welcome to TikTok's thrilling world! In this chapter, we'll start your TikTok adventure with the first step: establishing your TikTok account.

How to Make a TikTok Account: Your Path to Fame and Fortune

You've certainly seen a slew of viral TikTok videos and want to make your own. The good news: it's simpler than you think! First and foremost, get the TikTok app from your favorite app store. Once it's installed, here's how you set up your account and launch your TikTok career:

1. Sign Up Using Your Phone or Email

TikTok features a simple sign-up process. You may log in using your phone number, email address, or existing social network accounts such as Facebook or Google. Choose the finest choice for you, and you're one step closer to being a TikTok sensation!

2. Create Your Profile

On this colorful network, your TikTok profile is your digital presence, brand, and identity. Select a memorable username that expresses your personality or specialty. Your profile image and bio are both vital; they should communicate who you are. Let the world know right away if you're a cook, a comedian, a dancer, or a pet lover.

3. Investigate the TikTok Interface

Once you've logged in, spend some time exploring the app. Swipe through the For You Page (FYP) to get an idea of the type of material that is popular. Follow producers you respect and keep an eye out for the sorts of videos that pique your interest. TikTok is all about trends and originality, so keep an eye out for ideas.

4. Become acquainted with TikTok's features

TikTok provides a wealth of creative options for enhancing your videos. There are no restrictions on what you may do, from filters and effects to text and stickers. Experiment to find your style. Perhaps you like the slow-motion effect for your dancing films, or you prefer humorous voiceovers for your comedy skits. The more you experiment, the more your creativity will emerge.

5. Begin Making Your First TikTok Video

Are you feeling inspired? It's finally time to make your first TikTok video! Allow your imagination to flow, whether it's a lip-sync performance, culinary instruction, a witty comedy, or even an adorable pet moment. Don't stress about being flawless; the most important thing is to be yourself. Be yourself, have fun, and let your personality show through.

Congratulations! You've just begun your journey across the TikTok cosmos. After you've created your account, it's time to go further into the art of creating interesting TikTok videos. Buckle in, because the keys to creating content that not only attracts attention but keeps your viewers coming back for more will be revealed in the next chapters. Prepare to let your imagination run wild and leave your imprint on TikTok!

Navigating the TikTok Interface

Welcome to TikTok's heart: the vivid, ever-changing interface that acts as your canvas for creation. Understanding how to navigate this dynamic platform is vital for learning the art of TikTok. Let's take a guided tour of the UI so you can begin your TikTok journey with confidence.

1. Home Feed: TikTok's Heartbeat

The For You Page (FYP), also known as the Home Feed, is where the magic happens. It's a never-ending stream of videos personalized specifically to you. You'll find a mix of popular challenges, amusing sketches, life tips, and more here. Because the computer learns your preferences, the more you interact, the more personalized your feed gets.

2. Learn: Where Trends Take Flight

The Discover option, indicated by a magnifying glass, is your pass to discovering the most recent TikTok trends. This is where you can find popular hashtags, challenges, and content from producers all across the world. Dive in, get inspired, and don't be scared to participate in the newest viral challenges - it's a great way to increase your profile.

3. Follow: Your Social Circle

You'll discover videos from the producers you follow on the Following tab, which is symbolized by a silhouette icon. These individuals might be friends, influencers, celebrities, or companies. Engage with their material by commenting, liking, and sharing - developing a network on TikTok is essential for generating a supportive community around your content.

4. Direct Connections Inbox

Your communication center is the Inbox symbol, which is commonly shaped like a speech bubble. You'll get alerts for likes, comments, following, and mentions here. Respond to comments and messages from your audience to engage them - making a true relationship with your viewers improves your TikTok experience.

5. Using the '+' Button to Record Your Video

The '+' button, located at the bottom center of the screen, is your entry point to producing content. When you tap it, you'll be sent to TikTok's recording interface. You may set the length of your movie, add effects, alter the pace, and insert sounds from TikTok's wide collection here. Experiment with various effects, soundtracks, and transitions to make your films more visually appealing and entertaining.

6. *Profile: Your Online Identity*

Your TikTok journey is displayed in your Profile, which is represented by a silhouette or a profile image. Customize your profile image, write an interesting bio, and include your greatest videos in the Featured area. Make your profile appealing and expressive of your personality or brand; it is your digital identity.

You're ready to start exploring, participating, and, most importantly, creating now that you've been acquainted with the TikTok interface! Remember that TikTok is a platform for having fun, expressing yourself, and connecting with others. So embrace your creative side, immerse yourself in the latest trends, and let your imagination run wild. You now have access to the TikTok cosmos; go forth and conquer it!

Setting Up Your Profile for Success

Your TikTok profile is more than simply a digital placeholder; it serves as your platform, your brand's shop, and your passport to the TikTok spotlight. The first step toward success on this platform is to create an appealing and honest profile. Here's how to build up your profile to make an impact and gain a loyal following.

1. Select the Appropriate Profile Picture

The first thing people see about you is your profile image. Whether it's your enthusiastic face, your business emblem, or a visually appealing image, make sure it successfully reflects you or your brand. Choose something distinct, memorable, and reflects your personality or expertise.

2. Write a Captivating Bio

Your bio serves as your elevator pitch to the TikTok community. Convey who you are and what you do in a restricted character area. Are you a fitness fanatic, a foodie, a travel blogger, or a good storyteller? Be succinct, humorous, and sincere. Emojis may offer a whimsical touch, but keep them to a minimum.

Remember that clarity is essential; let readers know what to anticipate from your material.

3. Connect Your Other Social Media Accounts

Connect your TikTok profile to your Instagram, YouTube, or Twitter accounts. This multi-platform presence not only broadens your reach but also increases your reputation. People are more inclined to follow you if they notice you are active on several platforms. It also makes it easy for your TikTok followers to locate your work elsewhere.

4. Showcase Your Best Content

Your profile's Featured section is premium real estate. It should be curated using your most interesting and representative videos. These might be your most popular projects, videos showcasing your ability, or content exemplifying your style. When people visit your profile, these films are your opportunity to make a good first impression.

5. Exhibit Your Skills and Interests

Being multi-dimensional is advantageous in the TikTok universe. If you have a variety of hobbies or abilities, don't be afraid to show them out. Let your audience know what you're enthusiastic about, whether it's cooking, dancing, DIY crafts, or tech reviews. You may attract followers who share your interests, resulting in the formation of a committed community around your material.

6. Remain Consistent

Building a brand on TikTok requires consistency. Maintain a similar theme or design across your profile, from your profile photo to your bio and the information you provide. This isn't to say you can't evolve; just make sure there's a thread that connects your profile. A consistent profile generates a distinctive brand image, increasing the likelihood that people will remember and follow you.

Make your TikTok profile a vivid, genuine, and inviting canvas. It's the portal via which visitors join your universe, so make it one they can't help but open. A well-crafted profile lays the groundwork for a solid TikTok presence, laying the groundwork for your quest to becoming a TikTok phenomenon. So, go ahead and inject your personality, creativity, and one-of-a-kindness into your profile, and let the TikTok journey begin!

Chapter 2

Content Creation Strategies

Identifying Your Niche and Audience

Creating content for TikTok is more than just hurling films into the digital void; it's about forging a genuine relationship with your audience. To do so effectively, you must first establish your specialty and understand your target audience. Your specialization, enthusiasm, and distinct point of view all contribute to your niche. It is what distinguishes you in the wide TikTok landscape.

1. Identify Your Passion

What causes your heart to pound? What could you possibly speak about indefinitely? Your passion is your compass, directing you to a specialization that matches your interests. Your passion will fuel your creativity and authenticity, whether it's fitness, fashion, technology, humor, or even specialized themes like antique book collecting or sustainable living.

2. Research and Exploration

TikTok allows you to see what's popular, what others are talking about, and what interests you. Understand the newest trends, popular hashtags, and what material connects with visitors by researching your area. While being loyal to your passion, staying on top of trends allows you to inject relevancy into your material.

3. Identify Your Audience

Understanding your target audience is critical. Who exactly are they? What are their passions? What difficulties do they face? Customize your content to meet their needs and tastes. If your specialty is fitness, for example, your audience may include health-conscious folks seeking training advice. Knowing your target audience allows you to develop content that speaks directly to them, resulting in a deeper bond.

Crafting Engaging TikTok Videos

Creating interesting TikTok videos is a science as much as an art. It requires innovation, narrative, and an awareness of the platform's intricacies. Here's how to create videos that captivate viewers and make an impression.

1. Begin with a Hook

Capture your audience's interest within the first few seconds. A fascinating phrase, a surprising sight, or a brief glimpse of what's to come are all examples of enticing hooks. The hook establishes the tone and entices people to continue watching.

2. Tell Us a Story

Every amazing TikTok video, whether it's a 15-second comedy, a culinary demonstration, or a motivational speech, tells a narrative. Make a story arc with a beginning, middle, and end. Make viewers laugh, weep, or ponder by emotionally engaging them. A fascinating tale holds viewers' attention.

3. Visual Appeal

TikTok is a visual social media network. Make use of eye-catching images, rich colors, and inventive transitions. Experiment with the effects, filters, and editing tools available on TikTok. Visually appealing videos are more likely to be shared and remembered.

4. Selection of Soundtrack

The mood is set by music. Choose music that enhances your material. The correct soundtrack enhances the viewer's experience, whether it's exciting music for dynamic dancing videos or relaxing melodies for cookery demos.

5. Interact with Your Audience

Encourage viewers to participate. Create polls, ask questions, and reply to comments. Engaging with your audience fosters a sense of belonging. Viewers are more likely to become devoted followers if they feel heard and respected.

6. Consistency is Essential

Familiarity grows from consistency. Post frequently, but keep the quality of your content high. Establish a posting plan that works for you, whether it's daily, a few times a week, or weekly. Consistent content keeps your audience interested and looking forward to your next upload.

You build the route for TikTok success by establishing your specialty, knowing your audience, and mastering the art of creating entertaining videos. Remember that TikTok is a site where there are no rules. So, let your creativity go wild, try out new styles, and most importantly, have fun. The TikTok universe awaits your distinct voice; go ahead and make it known, one engaging video at a time.

Incorporating Trends and Challenges

TikTok's lifeblood is trends and problems. They are the platform's collective heartbeat, defining its culture and fuelling creativity. Mastering the skill of incorporating trends and problems into your films as a content creator may greatly increase your exposure and engagement. Here's how to ride the viral wave and make trends work for you.

1. Remain Trend-Aware

TikTok trends may be as strong as they are transitory. Explore the 'Discover' area on a regular basis to stay on top of popular hashtags, challenges, and formats. Participate in niche-related challenges. Trends have a wide appeal, which allows you to reach new audiences and get followers that share your interests.

2. Add Your Own Personal Touch

While keeping up with trends is important, putting your own spin on them is what makes your material stand out. Incorporate your individuality and style into any activity, whether it's a dancing competition, a cooking trend, or a comedy sketch. Your uniqueness is your most valuable asset; it is what helps visitors remember you in the middle of a sea of identical information.

3. Time is of the Essence

Take advantage of trends early, but keep in mind their lifetime. Some trends last a long time, while others disappear fast. Your exposure might be increased by timing your engagement. If you catch a rising trend, you may be able to ride its apex and achieve significant traction.

Utilizing TikTok's Editing Tools

The editing capabilities on TikTok are your secret weapon for turning ordinary videos into mesmerizing masterpieces. From filters and effects to transitions and text, these tools may help you enhance and aesthetically appeal to your material. Here's how to use TikTok's editing capabilities to your advantage.

1. Experiment with Filters and Effects

TikTok provides a plethora of filters and effects to spice up your videos. There's something for everyone, from face-altering effects to artistic filters. Experiment with different filters to see which ones improve your content. Effects may add drama, comedy, or intrigue to your presentation; utilize them imaginatively to keep your audience engaged.

2. Master Transitions

Transitions between scenes that are smooth may make your films seem polished and professional. You may use TikTok's editing suite to create smooth transitions between footage. Mastering transitions, whether it's a basic cut, a dissolve, or a creative transition effect, can improve the flow of your movies and keep viewers engaged from start to finish.

3. Incorporate Text and Captions

Text may be used to provide context, levity, or focus to your films. To express your point, use text and captions wisely. Well-placed text may improve the viewer's knowledge and engagement, whether it's humorous one-liners, helpful subtitles, or interesting questions.

4. Utilize TikTok's Sound Library

The enormous music collection of TikTok is a goldmine for content makers. Music creates atmosphere and can elicit feelings. Enhance your films with famous music, sound effects, or even viral audio snippets. To create a harmonic viewing experience, sync your material with the pace and mood of the chosen sound.

5. Try out the Stitch and Duet Features

You may collaborate with other producers or comment to their material using TikTok's Stitch and Duet capabilities. These characteristics provide limitless opportunities for creative collaboration and fascinating narrative. Whether you're bringing your own spin to a famous video or working with another artist, these tools can help you reach new audiences.

Incorporating trends and understanding TikTok's editing tools are critical abilities that may completely improve your TikTok adventure. By being trend-aware, integrating your distinct style, and creatively employing editing capabilities, you not only keep your material new and engaging, but you also establish yourself as a creative force on TikTok. So, embrace the trends, immerse yourself in the editing tools, and let your imagination run wild. Your next viral hit might be only a trend away!

Chapter 3

Building Your TikTok Brand

Establishing Your Unique Brand Identity

In the fast-paced world of TikTok, where material abounds, having a distinct brand identity is your key to distinguishing out. Your brand is more than simply a logo or a clever name; it is the heart of your content, the essence of who you are. Here's how to build out your specialty and create a brand identity that connects with your target audience.

1. Identify Your Core Values

Your brand is a reflection of your core principles. What do you hold dear? What is your intended message? Your basic beliefs shape your content, whether it's about sustainability, innovation, comedy, or sincerity. Align your videos with these ideals for authenticity and to attract people who share your ideas.

2. Create a Consistent Visual Style

Brand recognition is created via visual consistency. Maintain a consistent visual design, from your profile image to the colors and filters you employ in your movies. Whether it's a warm, antique tone or a colorful, modern palette, your images should represent the personality of your company. Consistency develops familiarity, helping your content stand out in a sea of videos.

3. Create a Distinctive Voice

The personality of your brand is defined by your writing style, sense of humor, and tone of voice. Are you clever and caustic, or welcoming and warm? Find a tone that works for your audience and stick to it. A distinct voice makes your content memorable and humanizes your brand.

Collaborations and Partnerships

TikTok's success is built on collaborations and partnerships. By collaborating with other producers or businesses, you not only broaden your audience but also offer new views and innovation to your work. Here's how you use collaborations and partnerships to boost your TikTok brand.

1. Select Compatible Partners

Look for creators or companies who share your ideals. Compatibility creates authenticity, resulting in real and compelling interactions. Shared values form the cornerstone of successful collaborations, whether with a fellow content producer, a company in your specialty, or a cause you believe in.

2. Create Win-Win Partnerships

Collaboration should be advantageous to both parties. Consider innovative methods to combine the capabilities of both sides. It might be a duet, a team competition, or a live session co-hosted by both parties. Collaborations that benefit both parties increase the reach of your content while introducing your business to a new audience.

3. Remain Transparent and Genuine

Transparency fosters trust. Be upfront about cooperation; your audience values candor. A genuine passion for your partner's content or items comes over and is well received by viewers. Authenticity increases the credibility of your business and builds a devoted community.

4. Utilize Cross-Promotion

Cross-promotion is an effective tactic. Promote your partnerships on social media and urge the collaborator to do the same. This cross-pollination exposes your brand to a wider range of people, improving your following and engagement.

Building your TikTok brand is a never-ending journey of self-discovery, creativity, and connection. By developing a distinct brand identity and welcoming partnerships, you not only generate great content but also cultivate a community that believes in your message. Remember that your brand is more than what you say; it is also what you do, how you connect, and the effect you make. Allow your business to shine, cooperate genuinely, and watch your TikTok presence skyrocket!

Growing Your Follower Base Organically

Growing your TikTok following base is about creating a dedicated audience that likes your content, not just statistics. Organic growth, albeit modest, is long-term and results in engaged followers who are more inclined to support your path. Here's how you expand your TikTok following naturally.

1. Consistently High-Quality Content
Consistency is essential, but it must be accompanied by quality. Posting high-quality, engaging material regularly keeps your audience interested and returning for more. Experiment, listen to your audience's input, and gradually develop your content approach.

2. Interact with Your Audience
Engagement requires both parties to participate. Participate in discussions, respond to comments, and like and share stuff from your followers. When your audience feels heard and respected, they are more inclined to engage with your content and share it with others.

3. Partnership with Other Creators
Collaborations help your work reach new audiences. You may acquire visibility by collaborating with other authors and tapping into their fan base. Collaborations

frequently result in cross-promotion, allowing both sides to naturally increase their following.

4. Take Part in Challenges and Trends

Participating in challenges and trends keeps your material relevant while also exposing it to a larger audience. Trending hashtags and challenges are frequently seen. When you participate in popular trends, you boost your chances of getting discovered by users who are interested in those trends.

Monetizing Your TikTok Account

Making money from your TikTok love is an amazing milestone in your path. TikTok has many monetization options, letting you profit from your creativity and influence. Here's how to properly monetize your TikTok account.

1. Become a member of the TikTok Creator Fund

The TikTok Creator Fund allows you to earn money based on the performance of your videos. As your following and views increase, you will be able to join the Creator Fund. TikTok compensates creators depending on their interaction numbers, ensuring a consistent cash stream.

2. Brand Collaborations and Sponsorships

Brands are constantly on the search for powerful TikTok producers to advertise their products or services. Brands may contact you for collaborations as your follower count develops. Alternatively, you might approach brands in your specialty and explore partnership opportunities. Choosing relationships that are authentic to your audience is critical.

3. Offering Products or Merchandise

TikTok provides a platform for showcasing and selling your items, commodities, or services. TikTok's engaged audience might be a prospective consumer base for artwork, fashion, or digital items. TikTok's features, such as the Shop Now button, may be used to bring viewers to your online business or website.

4. Live Donations and Gifts

During live streaming, TikTok Live fans may give gifts and money to their favorite creators. During live streams, interact with your audience by hosting Q&A sessions or providing unique behind-the-scenes footage. Viewers frequently enjoy the ability to personally support creators through gifts and donations.

Growing your organic following base and monetizing your TikTok account are two interwoven activities. Your monetization potential grows as you create an active community. Remember that retaining authenticity, connecting with your audience authentically, and generating material that connects with your viewers' interests are the keys to effective monetization. By achieving this balance, you can transform your TikTok obsession into a long-term source of money while still inspiring and entertaining your fans.

Chapter 4

For Businesses: TikTok Marketing Tactics

Creating Effective TikTok Ad Campaigns

TikTok stands out as a digital marketing powerhouse for firms looking to reach a large and engaged audience in an ever-changing marketplace. It takes more than merely showcasing things to create a great TikTok marketing campaign; it takes conveying an engaging tale, catching attention, and creating meaningful interaction. Here's how to design TikTok marketing campaigns that have an impact.

1. Know Your Audience

Understand your TikTok target demographic before getting into ad production. What are their passions? What difficulties do they face? Ad content that is tailored to your target audience will result in increased engagement rates. TikTok's broad user base allows you to reach out to a wide range of demographics, so narrow down your target audience.

2. *Utilize TikTok's Ad Formats*

TikTok has a variety of ad types to fit various marketing objectives:

- **In-Feed Advertisements:** These advertisements mix in with authentic material in consumers' feeds. Create interesting films that catch consumers' attention in the first few seconds and encourage them to participate or learn more.

- **Branded Hashtag Contests:** Branded challenges may be used to encourage user involvement. Create a memorable, easy-to-follow challenge and publicize it via influencers or sponsored hashtags. User-generated content increases brand trust and engagement.

- **Branded Effects:** Create bespoke AR effects for users to utilize in their films. Branded effects raise brand awareness and inspire people to interact creatively with your products.

- **TopView Advertisements:** When users launch the app, these full-screen adverts display, ensuring maximum visibility. Create aesthetically beautiful and succinct videos that successfully deliver your message.

3. Tell an Engaging Story

TikTok consumers enjoy emotional storylines. Create an engaging narrative for your brand or product. Create an emotional connection by using realistic personalities, comedy, or motivating words. A captivating tale inspires visitors to share and interact with your material.

4. Interact with TikTok Trends

Keep up with TikTok trends and apply them to your advertising strategies. Make use of popular songs, challenges, or topics that are relevant to your business. Trend-related material appears current and relatable, boosting the probability that people will interact with your ad.

5. Partner with TikTok Influencers

Influencers wield considerable power on TikTok. Collaborate with influencers whose followers are similar to those of your target audience. Influencers may include your items in their content with ease, giving authenticity and credibility. Genuine recommendations from influencers boost trust and increase conversions.

6. *Track, Analyze, and Optimize*

Use TikTok's analytics tools to track the success of your marketing campaign. Keep track of analytics like views, engagement rates, and conversions. Analyze user input and modify your plan as needed. A data-driven strategy allows you to fine-tune your efforts, assuring the best possible outcomes and return on investment.

Creating great TikTok ad campaigns involves innovation, audience comprehension, and a pulse on TikTok trends. Businesses can harness the full potential of TikTok's vast user base by crafting compelling stories, utilizing diverse ad formats, collaborating with influencers, leveraging data-driven insights, capturing attention, driving engagement, and ultimately achieving marketing success in the digital age.

Leveraging Influencer Marketing on TikTok

Influencer marketing has arisen as a potent technique in the dynamic world of social media, and it's an art form on TikTok. Using influencers helps organizations reach out to pre-existing, engaged audiences while benefiting from the authenticity and trust that influencers have built. Here's how you can use TikTok's influencer marketing to boost your brand's visibility.

1. Find the Right Influencers

A great campaign is built on selecting the appropriate influencers. Look for influencers whose content is consistent with the ideals, target audience and goods of your company. The importance of authenticity cannot be overstated; true congruence between the influencer's specialty and your brand enables an organic integration that connects with viewers.

2. Embrace Diverse Influencer Collaborations

TikTok has a wide range of influencers, ranging from mega-celebrities to micro-influencers. Mega-influencers may reach millions of people and provide enormous exposure. In contrast, micro-influencers frequently have highly engaged specialized audiences. Consider combining both for a more thorough strategy. Because of their actual ties with followers, micro-influencers in particular may generate extraordinarily high engagement rates.

3. Promote Creativity and Liberty

Influencers thrive on original material, and TikTok is all about it. Allow influencers to display your product or service in a way that suits their style. Authenticity shows through when influencers easily integrate your brand into their content, allowing their personality to blend flawlessly with your product.

4. Take Advantage of TikTok's Distinctive Features

TikTok has a variety of interactive elements, including challenges, duets, and stitches. Collaborate with influencers to develop branded challenges or encourage them to join current trends in your niche. TikTok's interactive aspects enable influencers to actively connect with their audience, increasing the reach of your business.

5. Enable Real Reviews and Testimonials

Genuine reviews are equally as important as showy endorsements in influencer marketing. Encourage influencers to offer unbiased feedback about your product or service. Authenticity fosters audience trust, resulting in a more responsive client base.

6. Determine the Impact and ROI

Use TikTok's analytics tools to assess the effectiveness of your influencer marketing. Keep track of the campaign's interaction rates, video views, and follower development. Track sales, website visits, and other key performance indicators (KPIs) that are impacted by the influencer partnership. Insights from data can help you fine-tune your influencer marketing approach for future campaigns.

7. Create Long-Term Relationships

Influencer marketing is more than simply a one-time tactic; it is about developing long-term relationships. Invest in cultivating relationships with influencers who are truly interested in your business. Long-term collaborations build authenticity because influencers become true brand champions, making their endorsements even more powerful.

Using TikTok influencer marketing goes beyond transactional advertisements; it's about making meaningful connections with the platform's audience.

Businesses can leverage the true storytelling power of influencers, driving their brand to new heights in the lively TikTok community, by selecting the proper influencers, fostering creativity, using interactive features, and analyzing the effect.

Utilizing Hashtags and Challenges for Brand Promotion

TikTok's pulse is paced by hashtags and challenges. These interactive components not only define the platform's culture but also function as effective brand marketing tools. When used correctly, hashtags and challenges may propel your business into the spotlight, reaching millions of interested people. Here's how to master the art of using hashtags and challenges to promote your company on TikTok.

1. Craft Personalized Hashtags

Create a distinct and memorable customized hashtag that captures the soul of your company. A branded hashtag, whether it's your brand name, a snappy slogan, or a word linked with your products, functions as your digital signature. Encourage viewers to utilize your brand's hashtag while generating content about it. Branded hashtags not only build a community but also make tracking user-generated material linked with your business simple.

2. Be a part of TikTok Trends

TikTok trends change quickly, and jumping on current trends may increase your brand's visibility. Keep up with popular hashtags and challenges in your niche. Participating in popular trends not only exposes your brand to a larger audience but also demonstrates its relevance and innovation.

3. Start Branded Challenges

Branded challenges are an excellent method to keep TikTok's active user base engaged. Make a challenge that corresponds to your brand's message or products. Make the task enjoyable, simple to complete, and aesthetically appealing. Engage influencers or celebrities to help you launch your challenge. TikTok users like taking part in challenges, which provides the potential for your brand to go viral as consumers passionately engage.

4. Encourage Participation by Users

For brand promotion, user-generated material is a goldmine. Encourage consumers to utilize your branded hashtag to produce content relating to your brand. Host challenges that encourage customers to be creative while utilizing your items. Engage with user inputs to acknowledge and thank them, establishing a feeling of community around your business.

5. Utilize TikTok Ads with Hashtags

Incorporate your company's hashtags into TikTok advertising. Make aesthetically engaging advertising using your branded hashtag to encourage people to engage and participate. When consumers see your branded hashtag in an advertisement, they are more likely to remember it, which leads to more user-generated content and engagement in your challenges.

6. Track and Amplify

Track the performance of your branded hashtags and challenges with TikTok's analytics tools. Keep track of the number of times your hashtags have been viewed, user interaction, and user-generated material. Determine what works best and expand on successful initiatives. Consider including user-generated material on your brand's page to highlight your vibrant and engaged community.

Understanding how to use hashtags and challenges on TikTok requires originality, relevancy, and interaction. Businesses can harness the viral dynamics of TikTok by creating catchy branded hashtags, participating in trends, launching engaging challenges, encouraging user participation, integrating hashtags into ads, and analyzing performance. This fosters a community-driven approach to brand promotion and creates lasting brand resonance in the vibrant TikTok ecosystem.

Chapter 5

For Creators and Influencers: Maximizing Earnings

Understanding TikTok's Creator Fund

As a TikTok creator or influencer, your creativity has the potential to generate a consistent income. TikTok's Creator Fund is one such way to directly monetize your material. Understanding how to successfully utilize this money will considerably increase your earnings.

1. Application and Eligibility

To be eligible for TikTok's Creator Fund, you must be at least 18 years old, have over 100,000 followers, and constantly create compelling content. Once you've determined your eligibility, you may apply for the Creator Fund via your TikTok profile settings.

2. Potential Earnings

The Creator Fund estimates payouts depending on your video performance, including views, interaction, and audience geography. The more views and interactions your films acquire, the more money you'll make. To optimize your profits from the Creator Fund, focus on providing high-quality, engaging content.

3. Continuity and Quality

The Creator Fund places a premium on consistency. Posting high-quality material regularly not only keeps your audience interested but also helps your revenue. The Creator Fund will pay you more if you constantly produce and connect with your audience.

Negotiating Brand Deals and Sponsorships

Negotiating commercial partnerships and sponsorships is a profitable route for artists and influencers outside of the Creator Fund. Navigating these collaborations successfully needs dexterity, expertise, and deep knowledge of your worth as a content developer.

1. Know Your Value

Recognize the value you provide to brands. Your worth is determined by factors such as your following count, engagement rate, niche relevancy, and creative style. Investigate industry norms and negotiate charges that reflect your clout and the value you provide to the company.

2. Authenticity is Crucial

Maintain your partnerships' honesty. Choose brands that reflect your ideals and are appealing to your target audience. Genuine endorsements are more persuasive to viewers and increase brand reputation. Your genuine interest in a product or service shows through, amplifying the impact of your sponsored content.

3. Professional Communication

Negotiations should be approached with professionalism. Define expectations, deliverables, and remuneration conditions clearly. Contracts or written agreements are required to ensure that both parties are aware of their respective duties and obligations. Professionalism generates trust and long-term brand partnerships.

4. Diverse Partnerships

Diversify your brand collaborations to meet the needs of diverse segments of your audience. Collaborate with businesses that cater to a wide range of interests within your specialty. This diversity not only increases your revenue but also broadens the attraction of your material to a larger audience.

5. Monitor Your Impact

Monitor the effectiveness of your sponsored content. If appropriate, track engagement metrics, audience comments, and sales data. Providing real outcomes for companies proves the efficacy of your influence, enhancing your worth for future collaborations.

A systematic strategy is required to maximize your revenue as a producer or influencer. You can turn your creative journey into a viable and sustainable enterprise by understanding TikTok's Creator Fund, negotiating brand deals professionally, being authentic, diversifying relationships, and measuring your effect. Remember that your creativity and influence are extremely valuable, and with the appropriate techniques, you can transform your passion into a flourishing TikTok profession.

Selling Merchandise and Products on TikTok

Selling gear and products on TikTok is more than just a transaction; it's a chance to interact with your audience on a more personal level and provide them with something tangible that symbolizes your business. Here's how to sell stuff and products on TikTok efficiently.

1. Create Engaging Product Content

Display your products in unique and aesthetically attractive ways. To make compelling product videos, use TikTok's tools such as transitions, filters, and effects. Highlight your items' distinctive qualities, illustrate how they may be utilized, and give client testimonials. The more fascinating and authentic your product content, the more likely your audience will buy.

2. Utilize Shoppable Features

TikTok contains shoppable capabilities, which enable users to make purchases straight from the platform. Incorporate elements such as the Shop Now button and product tags into your movies. Connect your online store or product pages to these capabilities, allowing users to easily browse and purchase your items with a few clicks.

3. Hold Limited-Time Offers and Flash Sales

Create a feeling of urgency and excitement for your TikTok audience by holding limited-time deals and flash sales. During these events, provide discounts, bundles, or exclusive items. Limited-time promotions drive impulse purchases and generate discussion among your followers.

4. Respond to Customer Feedback

Encourage customers to provide feedback and discuss their experiences with your products. Engage with their remarks, answer their queries, and express gratitude for their assistance. Positive interactions foster trust and improve the reputation of your brand, resulting in more pleased consumers and repeat business.

Engaging with Your Fanbase for Continuous Support

Your TikTok following is at the heart of your success. Engaging with people is about developing a real and devoted community that supports your journey, not just pushing items. Here's how to build a strong and supportive fanbase.

1. Interact and Respond Regularly
Respond to comments, ask questions, and hold Q&A sessions to interact with your audience. Demonstrate a genuine interest in their thoughts and experiences. Regular conversations build your audience's relationship with you by making them feel valued and appreciated.

2. Generate Exclusive Content
Make unique material available to your TikTok audience, such as behind-the-scenes videos, sneak peeks of new projects, or special instructions. Exclusive material gives your audience a sense of belonging and devotion by making them feel like insiders.

3. Host Fan Engagement Contests
Create challenges or contests just for your following. Encourage them to make content about your company or goods. Recognize and award the finest entries. Fan engagement challenges not only show off your followers'

inventiveness but also enhance their connection with your company.

4. Express Gratitude and Appreciation
Openly express your appreciation for your fans' support. Let your followers know how much you appreciate them, whether through shout-outs, thank-you letters, or fan appreciation videos. Genuine expressions of thanks foster a pleasant environment and promote ongoing support.

5. Come Together to Celebrate Milestones
Share your accomplishments and landmarks with your followers. Celebrate together when you reach a particular number of followers, launch a new product, or achieve a personal goal. The support of your supporters helps your success, and commemorating anniversaries increases their sense of belonging and pride.

Building a loyal fanbase and monetizing your TikTok impact requires a fine mix of product promotion and genuine engagement with your viewers. You can turn your TikTok presence into a vibrant community and a viable business endeavor by providing captivating product content, exploiting shoppable features, offering limited-time specials, and connecting with your following authentically. Remember that your followers are more than just clients; they are your devoted supporters, and fostering these bonds may lead to long-term success on TikTok and elsewhere.

Chapter 6

Navigating TikTok's Policies and Guidelines

Staying Compliant with TikTok's Rules

TikTok's rich and varied community flourishes inside a framework of rules and norms meant to keep all users safe and positive. Understanding and following to these standards is critical not just for the sustainability of your account, but also for maintaining a trustworthy online profile. Here's how to properly manage TikTok's regulations and standards.

1. Educate Yourself
Learn about TikTok's Community Guidelines and Terms of Service. These papers explain the platform's content, user behavior, and account management policies and expectations. TikTok's rules are often updated to meet developing concerns and trends, so please review them regularly.

2. Respect for Intellectual Property and Copyright

When generating content, make sure you have permission to use any music, photos, or other elements that appear in your movies. Copyright laws and intellectual property rights must be respected. Use TikTok's enormous music collection and editing capabilities to produce unique and interesting content while adhering to copyright guidelines.

3. Avoid Unsuitable Content

TikTok does not allow graphic, sexually suggestive, violent, discriminating, or dangerous content. Avoid using hate speech, harassing others, or encouraging risky behaviors. Maintaining positive, inclusive, and courteous material not only keeps you compliant but also creates a welcoming environment for your followers.

4. Protect Your Privacy

Respect both the privacy of others and your own. Personal information, addresses, phone numbers, and other sensitive data should not be included in your videos or comments. Obtain permission from anybody who appears in your recordings, especially if they are not famous characters. Privacy protection is essential for sustaining a secure online community.

5. Misinformation in Combat

TikTok's goal is to counteract disinformation and fake news. Before sharing information, double-check it, especially if it is about sensitive themes, health, or public events. Endorse unsubstantiated claims, conspiracy theories, or disinformation that may mislead your audience.

6. Keep an eye on comments and interactions

Keep an eye on the comments on your videos regularly. Any improper or disrespectful remarks should be removed or reported. Encourage pleasant interactions with your followers and set a good example. TikTok's comment filtering capabilities might help you manage your comment area more successfully.

7. Be Aware of Current Trends and Challenges

TikTok trends and difficulties can occasionally include dangerous activity. Before engaging in or supporting any challenge, use prudence and good judgment. Be mindful of the potential repercussions and make sure your participation adheres to TikTok's principles.

8. Make Use of Reporting Tools

If you come across something that violates TikTok's rules, you may report it using the platform's reporting tools. Reporting inappropriate content or abusive behavior helps to keep the community safe and respectful for all users.

9. Interact with Other Users Ethically

Respect other creators' work. Give credit when it is due, and avoid activities such as content theft, cyberbullying, or harassment. Ethical participation promotes a positive environment and positions you as a responsible member of the TikTok community.

By adhering to TikTok's policies and guidelines, you not only protect your account but also contribute to the platform's overall positive atmosphere. Being aware of the rules, staying informed, and encouraging respectful interactions not only ensures compliance but also allows you to be a positive influence within TikTok's diverse and creative community. Remember that being respectful and compliant on the platform increases your credibility, trustworthiness, and long-term success.

Handling Copyright and Intellectual Property Issues

TikTok's rich and diverse community flourishes under a framework of rules and principles meant to promote a safe and happy environment for all users. Understanding and following these standards is critical not just for the sustainability of your account, but also for maintaining a trustworthy online profile. Here's how to manage TikTok's regulations and standards efficiently.

1. Educate Yourself

Read TikTok's Community Guidelines and Terms of Service. These guidelines explain the platform's rules and expectations for content, user conduct, and account administration. TikTok's policies are updated regularly to reflect developing concerns and trends, so please review them regularly.

2. Respect Copyright and Intellectual Property

When generating content, make sure you have permission to use any music, photos, or other elements contained in your films. Respect copyright laws and intellectual property rights. Use TikTok's enormous music collection and editing capabilities to produce unique and compelling content while adhering to copyright regulations.

3. Avoid Inappropriate Content

TikTok forbids graphic, sexually suggestive, violent, discriminatory, or harmful material. Avoid using hate speech, harassing others, or encouraging risky actions. Making sure your material is uplifting, inclusive, and polite not only keeps you compliant but also creates a welcoming environment for your followers.

4. Protect Privacy

Respect the privacy of others as well as your own. Avoid including personal information, addresses, phone numbers, or any other sensitive data in your films or comments. Obtain permission from persons included in your videos, especially if they are not prominent personalities. Privacy protection is critical to sustaining a secure online environment.

5. Combat Misinformation

TikTok strives to stop the spread of disinformation and fake news. Verify information before sharing it, especially if it relates to sensitive themes, health, or public events. Be wary of embracing unproven claims, conspiracy theories, or disinformation that might mislead your audience.

6. Monitor Comments and Interactions

Monitor the comments on your videos regularly. Remove or report any improper or insulting remarks. Encourage constructive relationships among your followers and set a good example. TikTok's comment filtering options might help you manage the comment area more efficiently.

7. Be Aware of Trends and Challenges
Trends and challenges on TikTok can occasionally include dangerous activity. Before taking part in or promoting any challenge, use care and good judgment. Be mindful of the potential implications and ensure that your participation adheres to TikTok's rules.

8. Utilize Reporting Tools
Use the platform's reporting options if you come across content that violates TikTok's rules. Reporting improper content or abusive conduct helps to maintain a safe and courteous environment for all members.

9. Interact Ethically with Other Users
Respect the work of other creators. Give credit where it is due, and refrain from engaging in behaviors such as content theft, cyberbullying, or harassment. Ethical participation provides a pleasant environment and guarantees that you are viewed as a responsible member of the TikTok community.

By adhering to TikTok's laws and guidelines, you not only secure your account but also add to the platform's general pleasant vibe. Being aware of the rules, remaining educated, and cultivating courteous interactions not only ensures compliance but also allows you to be a constructive influence within TikTok's varied and creative community. Remember that being respectful and complying improves your credibility, trustworthiness, and long-term success on the platform.

Managing Online Etiquette and Cyberbullying

Understanding online etiquette and dealing with cyberbullying are vital skills in the digital environment, where words and acts may be amplified immediately. Respectfully navigating social encounters and dealing with unpleasantness with grace not only builds a great atmosphere for oneself but also sets an example for others. Here's how to efficiently handle online etiquette and confront cyberbullying on TikTok.

1. Maintain Good Online Etiquette

Treat people with the same respect and kindness that you expect. Avoid using derogatory words, hate speech, or personal insults. Constructive criticism is useful, but it must be delivered with courtesy and without animosity.

Practice Empathy: Understand and empathize with the experiences and viewpoints of others. Recognize that people come from a variety of backgrounds and cultures, which may impact their perspectives. Empathy promotes understanding and aids in the resolution of possible disputes.

Think Before You Post: Before posting any information or remark, pause and ponder. Consider how others could interpret your statements. Remember that once anything is posted online, it can be difficult to reverse the impact of nasty or harmful words.

Promote Positive Behavior:
Engage in encouraging discussions, congratulate people, and appreciate creativity to spread optimism. Encourage your followers to be polite and supportive. By maintaining a friendly atmosphere, you help to make the online experience more enjoyable for everyone.

2. Dealing with Cyberbullying

Recognize cyberbullying by doing the following: Be on the lookout for indicators of cyberbullying, such as abusive comments, threats, spreading rumors, or harassment. It is critical to distinguish between helpful and harmful criticism.

Do Not Engage: Avoid communicating with the bully if you face cyberbullying. Responding may worsen the problem. Instead, notify TikTok about the situation and block the person. Positive interactions and content development should be prioritized.

Report and Block: Use TikTok's reporting and banning tools. Any incidences of cyberbullying should be reported as soon as possible. TikTok has measures in place to investigate and prosecute users who violate community norms.

Supportive Community: Surround yourself with a supportive community. Encourage your followers to oppose cyberbullying. You may work together to create an environment where negativity is discouraged and compassion is rewarded.

Seek Help: If you are a victim of cyberbullying, don't be afraid to reach out to friends, family, or mental health specialists for help. Your well-being is important, and speaking with someone you trust may bring emotional comfort as well as practical counsel.

3. Encourage Digital Resilience

Develop Resilience: Develop resilience in the face of harsh criticism. Keep in mind that online exchanges frequently reflect the sender's problems rather than your merits. Rather than concentrating on the negative, focus on your passions and the good influence you make.

Educate Others: Educate your followers on proper online behavior and cyberbullying. Raise awareness about the consequences of online words and behaviors. You help to make the internet a safer place by cultivating an educated and compassionate community.

Managing online etiquette and dealing with cyberbullying necessitates a mix of empathy, digital resilience, and proactive measures. By promoting appropriate online conduct, detecting and responding to cyberbullying, and cultivating a supportive community, you help to create a respectful and encouraging environment on TikTok. Remember that your impact extends beyond your content; it influences the online environment for your fans and peers. You set a tremendous example for a more positive online environment by leading with compassion and empathy.

Chapter 7

Looking Ahead: TikTok Trends in 2024

Predictions and Forecasts for TikTok

As TikTok evolves, staying ahead of the curve is critical for creators, influencers, and companies looking to succeed on the platform. While the future is always dynamic and unexpected, studying existing patterns and new technology can give significant insights into the TikTok scene in 2024.

1. Augmented Reality (AR) Content's Rise

Although AR filters and effects are currently popular on TikTok, we may anticipate a considerable increase in the usage of augmented reality for generating interactive and immersive content by 2024. AR will be used by brands and artists to provide new experiences, letting consumers interact with products or stories in novel ways.

2. Social Responsibility and Sustainability

With environmental concerns gaining prominence throughout the world, TikTok is expected to witness an increase in content centered on sustainability, climate action, and social responsibility. Creators and enterprises who support environmental and social concerns will gain traction. Audiences are increasingly drawn to material that reflects their ideals, making socially responsible content a major trend.

3. Shopping via Livestream

TikTok is likely to gain traction in livestream shopping, which is currently popular in numerous Asian countries. This concept blends entertainment and e-commerce by allowing viewers to buy things while viewing live programming. This tool will be used by influencers and businesses to demonstrate items, answer questions, and provide an interactive shopping experience for their audience.

4. Educational Content in Short Form

As TikTok's audience expands, so will the demand for instructional programming. Short, interesting instructional, life hacks, and educational content presented in novel ways will gain popularity. Creators who can present essential information succinctly and engagingly will captivate audiences looking to acquire new skills and gain knowledge.

5. Micro-Influencers and Niche Communities

While mega-influencers have risen on TikTok, 2024 may see a move toward smaller, specialized groups and micro-influencers. These influencers will be appealing to marketers searching for true relationships since they have a committed and engaged following. TikTok's broad user base enables the emergence of several niche groups, opening up chances for producers with specialized interests.

6. Virtual Reality (VR) Content Integration

TikTok is planned to feature virtual reality material, providing users with immersive experiences. Audiences will be captivated by VR-enabled storytelling, gaming, and interactive excursions, offering new options for creative expression. Early adopters of VR technology will have a competitive advantage in engaging people in unique and interesting ways.

7. Continued Adoption of User-Generated Content

TikTok's appeal will continue to be centered on user-generated content. Algorithms on the site will continue to emphasize real and relatable material, encouraging people to share their stories, experiences, and creativity. TikTok's community-driven strategy will continue, so creators and companies must focus on forging true connections with their audience.

It is difficult to predict the exact future of a social media network, but these tendencies look at the probable routes TikTok may go in 2024. Creators and companies may survive in the dynamic and exciting world of TikTok by remaining agile, inventive, and in sync with the platform's developing features. Remember that the key is to remain inventive, sincere, and open to the next wave of creative ideas.

Adapting Your Strategies to Emerging Trends

Staying relevant and successful in TikTok's ever-changing landscape requires adaptability. As new features, content formats, and audience behaviors emerge, adapting your strategies becomes a necessity rather than a choice. Here's how to stay ahead of the competition by aligning your TikTok strategies with emerging trends.

1. Stay Informed and Inquisitive
Adopt a mindset of constant learning. Keep up to date on the latest TikTok updates, features, and trends. Attend webinars, follow TikTok influencers, and read industry reports. Curiosity about emerging trends is the foundation for effectively adapting your strategies.

2. Experiment with Different Formats
TikTok introduces new content formats regularly, such as live events, short challenges, and interactive features. Experiment with these formats to see what works best for your audience. Interactive polls, Q&A sessions, and behind-the-scenes peeks can boost your engagement.

3. Accept Ephemeral Content
Ephemeral content, which vanishes after a short period, is popular on social media platforms. TikTok Stories and

similar features allow for the creation of urgency and FOMO (Fear of Missing Out). Use these features for promotions, limited-time offers, and sneak peeks to effectively capture your audience's attention.

4. Take Advantage of TikTok's Shopping Features

TikTok's shopping features are evolving, including in-app stores and product catalogs. Keep up to date on e-commerce trends and use these features to showcase and sell your products directly to your target audience. Seamless shopping experiences can significantly increase your sales and brand loyalty.

5. Leverage the Strength of Niche Communities

TikTok's niche communities are thriving. Determine the micro-influencers and subcultures in your niche. Genuinely engage with these communities. To reach highly targeted audiences, work with micro-influencers. Understanding and catering to specific subcultures can result in devoted followers.

6. Accept User-Generated Content (UGC) Campaigns

User-generated content campaigns encourage your target audience to create content about your company or products. Use user-generated content (UGC) campaigns to build a sense of community and authenticity around your brand. Encourage and reward participants' creativity. UGC boosts engagement while also serving as social proof for your brand.

7. Put Social Responsibility and Sustainability First
Brands and creators are expected to be socially responsible as societal concerns grow. Demonstrate your dedication to social causes and sustainability. Share your eco-friendly practices and charitable initiatives openly. Audiences are more likely to interact with brands that share their values.

8. Data-Informed Decision Making
Use TikTok's analytics tools to learn more about your audience's behavior. Keep track of engagement metrics, popular content, and demographics of your followers. Use this data to fine-tune your content strategy, learn what works best, and adjust your approach as needed. Decisions based on data result in more effective strategies.

9. Network and Collaborate
Collaborate with other artists and brands. TikTok community networking can lead to new opportunities and collaborations. Participate in duos, challenges, and joint ventures. Collaborations not only broaden your reach but also expose you to new styles and formats of content.

Adapting your TikTok strategies to emerging trends necessitates a combination of creativity, curiosity, and strategic thinking. You can thrive in the ever-changing world of TikTok by staying informed, experimenting with new formats, embracing shopping features, engaging niche communities, encouraging user-generated content, demonstrating social responsibility, analyzing data, and collaborating effectively. Remember that adaptability is more than just following trends; it is also about innovating and leading the way in the ever-changing social media landscape.

Future-Proofing Your TikTok Presence

In the fast-paced world of social media, future-proofing your TikTok presence is about cultivating adaptability, authenticity, and resilience rather than predicting every change. By laying a solid foundation and staying on top of digital trends, you can position yourself to navigate the uncertainties and thrive in TikTok's ever-changing landscape.

1. Develop a Distinctive Brand Identity

Your anchor is your brand identity. Define what distinguishes you, your values, and your distinct style. Authenticity endures and is well-received by audiences. A genuine and consistent brand identity creates a lasting connection with your followers, making them more likely to stay engaged over time, whether you're a business or a creator.

2. Broaden Your Content and Skills

TikTok is an adaptable platform. Don't limit yourself to a single type of content or a specific niche. Experiment with various types of content, such as short skits and informative videos. Learn new skills, experiment with different trends, and be open to creative challenges. Diversifying your content keeps your audience engaged and attracts a larger audience.

3. Maintain Technological Agility

Technology advances at a breakneck pace. Keep up with the most recent gadgets, software, and editing tools. Learn about emerging technologies such as augmented reality, virtual reality, and artificial intelligence. Being technologically agile allows you to seamlessly incorporate new tools into your content, improving its quality and appeal.

4. Create a Community Rather Than Just an Audience

Create an authentic community around your content. Engage your followers, respond to comments, and create content that encourages interaction. A dedicated community can help you navigate platform changes and trends. They become your advocates, promoting your content and products.

5. Be Prepared for Algorithm Changes

Algorithms on social media are constantly evolving. Keep up to date on algorithm changes and adjust your content strategy accordingly. Pay attention to which content performs well, analyze audience feedback, and adjust your strategy accordingly. Being adaptable to algorithm changes ensures that your content reaches your target audience effectively.

6. Accept New Features and Formats

TikTok is constantly introducing new features and formats. Accept them as soon as possible. Integrating new features into your content, whether it's a new filter, interactive element, or content format, demonstrates your adaptability and keeps your content fresh and engaging.

7. Prioritize Long-Term Relationships

Prioritize long-term relationships with influencers and your audience if you're a business. Short-term trends pass, but genuine relationships endure. Long-term partnerships with influencers who share your brand's values, as well as cultivating customer loyalty, contribute to long-term success.

8. Track Industry Trends

Keep up to date on trends in your industry and related fields. Understanding broad market trends enables you to predict changes in consumer behavior. You position yourself as a forward-thinking creator or business by aligning your content or products with changing market demands.

9. Invest in Your Knowledge and Skills

Invest in your own personal and professional development. Enroll in classes, attend workshops, and read a lot. Continuously honing your skills and knowledge prepares you to take on new challenges and innovate in your content creation or business strategies.

Future-proofing your TikTok presence entails laying a solid foundation, remaining adaptable, and cultivating genuine connections. You can not only survive but thrive in TikTok's ever-changing landscape by cultivating a unique brand identity, diversifying your content, remaining technologically agile, building a supportive community, adapting to algorithm changes, embracing new features, focusing on long-term relationships, monitoring industry trends, and investing in your skills. Remember that the digital world rewards not only those who are willing to adapt, but also those who lead the change with creativity and authenticity.

Conclusion

Congratulations! This comprehensive guide on how to make money on TikTok in 2024 has come to an end. As you begin your TikTok journey or refine your existing strategies, keep in mind that success on this dynamic platform is about embracing your unique voice, creativity, and authenticity, not just following trends.

Key Takeaways Recap

1. Understanding TikTok Fundamentals: You've covered the fundamentals, from creating an account to mastering the TikTok interface.

2. Content Creation Strategies: Identifying your niche, creating engaging videos, and incorporating trends are critical to capturing the attention of your audience.

3. Building Your Brand: Creating a distinct identity, collaborating, and organically growing your follower base are all critical steps in developing a strong TikTok brand.

4. TikTok Marketing Strategies: You've investigated various avenues for businesses to succeed on TikTok, from effective ad campaigns to leveraging influencer marketing.

5. Monetization and Earnings Maximization: You've learned how to monetize your influence and maximize your earnings, whether through the Creator Fund, brand deals, or merchandise sales.

6. Navigating Policies and Etiquette: Understanding TikTok's policies, dealing with copyright issues, and managing online etiquette are all necessary for a positive online presence.

7. Responding to Emerging Trends: You can adapt to TikTok's changing landscape by staying informed, experimenting with new formats, and cultivating genuine connections.

8. Proofing Your Presence in the Future: To future-proof your TikTok presence, cultivate authenticity, diversify your content, embrace technology, build a community, and invest in your skills.

Insight and Motivation for TikTok Success in 2024

On TikTok, your potential is limitless. Remember that every successful TikTok creator or business began from the ground up. Accept your individuality, persevere, and never underestimate the power of authenticity.

TikTok in 2024 provides you with a platform to express your creativity, share your passions, connect with like-minded people, and even build a sustainable business. It's a platform where creativity is celebrated, and your ideas have the potential to reach millions.

Continue experimenting, learning, and, most importantly, enjoying the process as you navigate the trends and changes. TikTok is a community of creators and dreamers, not just a platform. Your journey here is about making a difference, sharing your story, and inspiring others, not just making money.

So go ahead and make that video, start that challenge, and start that business. Your success on TikTok in 2024 and beyond is a certainty, not a possibility. You're not just ready for TikTok with your passion, creativity, and knowledge; you're destined for TikTok success.

Here's to your TikTok journey in 2024, full of creativity, connection, and limitless possibilities. Accept it, enjoy it, and personalize it. Your TikTok adventure begins right now!

www.ingramcontent.com/pod-product-compliance
Lightning Source LLC
Chambersburg PA
CBHW062235290526
45794CB00006B/2292